Dedicated to
the awesome Olivia Mei...
singer, actor, writer, namer of Obo,
and master of chicken talk
at a very young age.
(buKaw!)

A Nanna & Obo Groovetoon ™
Illustrations - © 2025 Jaye Krebs
Words and music - © 2025 Jaye Krebs & Leora Cashe

oboPress
10986 82 Avenue, Delta, BC, Canada
www.nannaandobo.com/obopress

Scan and go to
NannaAndObo.com!

All rights reserved. No part of this book may be reproduced or transmitted in any means without permission in writing from the author or publisher, except by a reviewer, who may quote brief passages in a review.

ISBN: 978-1-0692893-1-5

... a chicken on her head!

She sent it on its way...

...it came back ...

...with a frilly dress below and a chicken on the top

(more fedora* than pet)

* fedora is another name for a hat!

Well, from that moment on the lady never left her friend.

... and luckily her wardrobe seemed to match...

...that chicken on her head!

That hen up in her hair,
it had a stylish flair!

She said, " A feather in your hat is the fashion,
so I've heard.
I think I'm going to wear...

...but they were whispering among themselves about...

...that chicken on her head!

It truly broke her heart!
She heard these fowl remarks...

Then one day, walking in the park, feeling sad and oh so blue,

She turned to smile a greeting but...

He was handsome!

He was tall...

...and on top of all...

...was a rooster on his head!

(cock-a-doodle-doo-dee!)

...with a little baby chicken on her head!

THE END

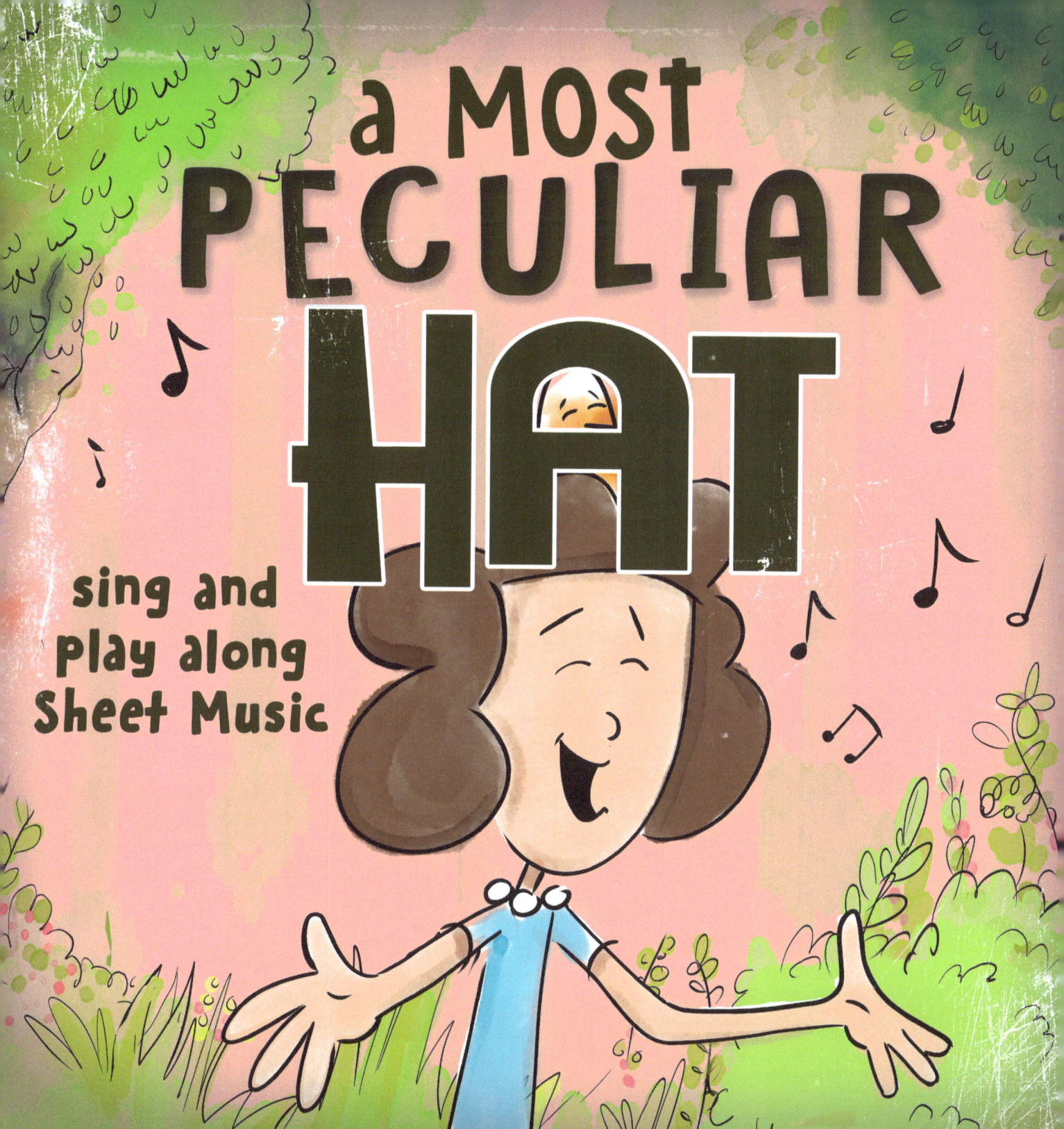

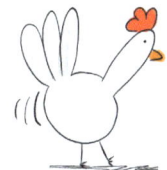

I want to tell a story so sit back in that chair
about a lovely lady quite absurd
it seemed peculiar she wore a chicken in her hair
A funny bouffant kinda bird

Well, on her walk each day old friends would smile and wave
ut they were whispering among themselves about that chicken on her head!

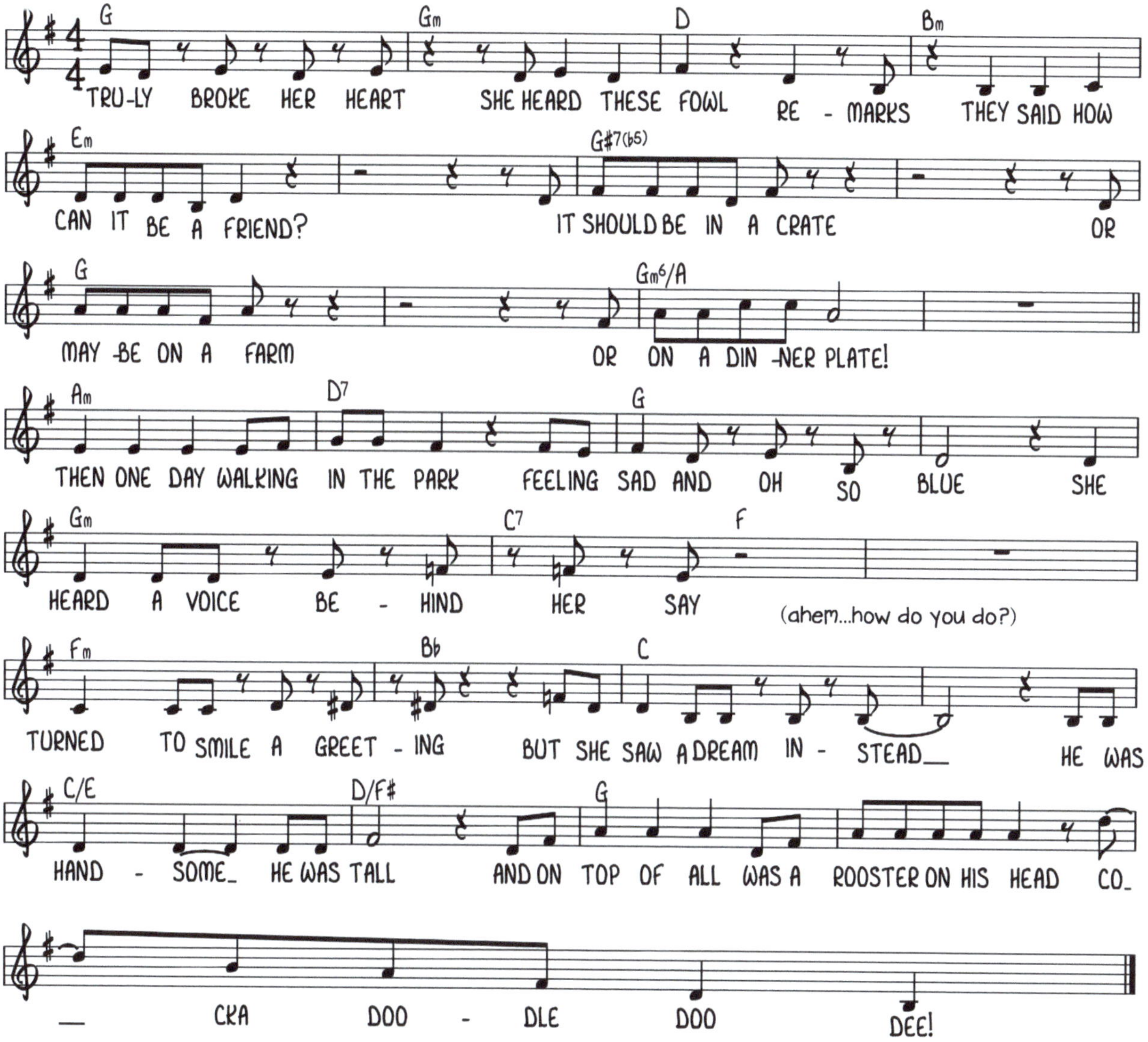
G Gm D Bm
TRU-LY BROKE HER HEART SHE HEARD THESE FOWL RE - MARKS THEY SAID HOW
Em G#7(b5)
CAN IT BE A FRIEND? IT SHOULD BE IN A CRATE OR
G Gm6/A
MAY BE ON A FARM OR ON A DIN - NER PLATE!
Am D7 G
THEN ONE DAY WALKING IN THE PARK FEELING SAD AND OH SO BLUE SHE
Gm C7 F
HEARD A VOICE BE - HIND HER SAY
(ahem...how do you do?)
Fm Bb C
TURNED TO SMILE A GREET - ING BUT SHE SAW A DREAM IN - STEAD__ HE WAS
C/E D/F# G
HAND - SOME_ HE WAS TALL AND ON TOP OF ALL WAS A ROOSTER ON HIS HEAD CO_
— CKA DOO - DLE DOO DEE!

Now to end this story with love all full in bloom
this foursome forms a fairly odd quartet
With a chicken on the bride and a rooster on the groom
happy ever after with a brand new baby girl...
with a little baby chicken on her head!

Hi there!
Thanks for reading or singing the book! Come on by **www.nannaandobo.com** for a visit!
Click on "music / audio" and you'll find the recorded version of "A Most Peculiar Hat"

The QR code will take you right to www.nannaandobo.com...you'll find Nanna & Obo Groovetoon videos, books, buttons, shirts, more sheet music and all sorts of fun stuff!

Drop us a note while you're there!

(Obo)

PS There are no AI generated images in this book. I drew and colored each picture... a lot of work and a lot of fun!

A Nanna & Obo Groovetoon ™
Illustrations © 2025 Jaye Krebs
Music and Lyrics © 2025 Jaye Krebs & Leora Cashe

oboPress
10986 82 Avenue, Delta, BC, Canada
www.nannaandobo.com/obopress

All rights reserved. No part of this book may be reproduced or transmitted in any means without permission in writing from the author or publisher, except by a reviewer, who may quote brief passages in a review.

ISBN: 978-1-0692893-1-5

Also by Jaye Krebs:

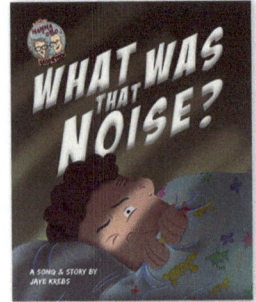

"...a good imagination
is a fantastic thing...
but sometimes..."

"...and kids will be crazy
a thousand years more!"

"...a fart can be a small thing...
or it can rearrange
your entire morning!"

www.ingramcontent.com/pod-product-compliance
Lightning Source LLC
Chambersburg PA
CBHW042123040426
42450CB00002B/47